SECRET
FOREST OF DEAN

Mark Turner

AMBERLEY

First published 2019

Amberley Publishing
The Hill, Stroud
Gloucestershire, GL5 4EP

www.amberley-books.com

ISBN 978 1 4456 8495 6 (print)
ISBN 978 1 4456 8496 3 (ebook)

British Library Cataloguing in Publication Data.
A catalogue record for this book is available from the
British Library.

Typesetting by Aura Technology and Software
Services, India. Printed in Great Britain.

Contents

Introduction

Gloucestershire's majestic Forest of Dean, with its estimated twenty million trees over 42 square miles of woodland, lies within a triangle between the River Severn on its east side and the famous Wye Valley on its west. The district, which spreads beyond the wooded area, has a long and interesting history, but much of this is relatively little known and many of its most fascinating buildings and structures are obscure or difficult to locate. This book seeks to pinpoint and describe the most significant aspects of the area's history and landscape, presenting the reader with a captivating and concise summary of much that might be termed 'secret'.

In geological terms, the district is founded on Palaeozoic rock created in a period between 225 and 600 million years ago, with one of the United Kingdom's smaller coalfields resting on the surface – iron ore deposits lying beneath and around this coalfield. Evidence of human habitation since at least the Bronze Age is provided by the presence of megalithic standing stones; several hill forts survive from the Iron Age, when ancient British tribes such as the Silures and Dobunni fought one another (as well as invaders from mainland Europe); and then, of course, there are numerous signs of Roman occupation in the Forest of Dean. The Romans set about exploiting the area's natural reserves, as illustrated by archaeological evidence of iron-smelting and coal-mining activities. The medieval period, too, saw much change in the Forest's landscape, especially following the Norman Conquest.

In the centuries following the Roman occupation the Forest was – since before the reign of William the Conqueror – owned by the Crown and was used mainly as a royal hunting ground. By the seventeenth century, however, it was primarily used to provide timber for the ships of the Royal Navy. It was in this century, too, that the district became the setting for military activity and conflict during the Civil War. From the eighteenth century, coal mining grew rapidly in the Forest as advantage was taken of deposits, producing millions of tons of coal and providing employment for many. For most of the district's inhabitants during this period, however, the Forest was a place of toil, danger and grinding poverty. Violent crime was far from unknown – indeed, Gloucestershire's only murders of police officers on duty occurred in the Forest in the nineteenth century.

A network of tramroads and railways through the Forest was created in the nineteenth century, mainly to serve local industry, but also to provide passenger services. As the twentieth century progressed, the economic mining of Forest coal became less and less viable, however, and by the mid-1960s the last of the big pits had closed. No longer financially sustainable, most of the Forest's railway lines, too, had been closed by the end of that decade. Today the district is – with its range of nature reserves, footpaths and cycle-ways, museums and heritage attractions – a popular base for visitors seeking to explore the ancient Forest and neighbouring Wye Valley. Many of these attractions have been imaginatively created from former industrial sites – such as coal mines, quarries and old railway trackbeds.

In the interests of completeness a fairly broad interpretation of the Forest of Dean's geographical area is used in this book. Although some writers have asserted that the Forest begins at the small town of Mitcheldean, on the east of the area, or that the Forest has never extended north of the town of Newent, all locations lying within today's Forest of Dean District Council's administrative area are included – even where some of these may seem somewhat remote from the Forest 'proper'. The various locations and features described follow a general pattern of 'virtual tours' beginning at the north of the district, and then continuing through the Forest's centre and alongside the Wye Valley, before heading south towards the River Severn and back up towards Gloucester.

Numerous people have been helpful and informative during my exploration of the Forest and preparation of this book. In particular, the following individuals have been especially supportive and enthusiastic: my good friends Stephen Clarke MBE and David Duruty de Lloyd; Mark Christopher; Rich Daniels MBE; Terry Hale; Mike Jackson; Robert 'Bif' Powell; my brother, Wakefield Turner (who photographed several of the relatively inaccessible locations); and Sheila White and Jonathan Wright. To these, and everyone who gave assistance, I extend sincere thanks and appreciation.

1. Ancient Monuments

Prehistory

Fossil remains found near the River Severn in 1952 indicate the presence of amphibian reptiles in what is now the Forest of Dean district, around 200 million years ago. The first evidence of human life, however, came in the form of man-made flint blades and scrapers of the later Paleolithic period that were discovered in the nineteenth century at King Arthur's Cave, between Monmouth and Symonds Yat. Although just outside Gloucestershire, this is very close to the Forest of Dean, suggesting that hunters of the late glacial period settled in or around the Forest.

Hunter-gatherers of the Mesolithic period and the later Neolithic period and Bronze Age colonised the wetlands of the Severn Estuary to the south of the Forest district, with traces of their hunting and fishing activities having been found in the silt and peat deposits of the low-lying coastal areas (known as the Levels) in the vicinity of Woolaston. Evidence that people of the Neolithic period were active in what is now the heart of the Forest was shown by the discovery of a Neolithic polished flint axe between Bream and St Briavels in 1989, while petrological examination of a Neolithic stone axe-head found at Viney Hill in 1955 revealed it to have come from Cumbria. Bronze Age axe-heads, too, have been found in the district, and a couple of round barrows at Blakeney were detected by a 1989 aerial survey. A barrow known locally as the 'Soldier's Tump' was excavated at Tiddenham Chase in the early 1950s, the finds being dated to the early Bronze Age.

The Forest's most visible Bronze Age monuments, however, are its two surviving standing stones. A solitary monolith of old red conglomerate known as the Long Stone stands to a height of 6 feet beside the Coleford road a little to the south-east of Staunton village, while a standing stone known as the Wibdon Broad Stone, some 9 feet in height, can be seen to the south-west of Woolaston, near the Severn Estuary and close to the railway line between Gloucester and South Wales. In the nineteenth century an ancient megalith called the Long Stone stood in a field between St Briavels and Bream, until in 1875 a farmer using gunpowder blew it to pieces.

The Iron Age peoples, who followed on from those of the Bronze Age, lived in organised tribal groups ruled by a chieftain – with conflict between opposing groups leading to the construction of hill forts, still commonly seen in Britain. A number of these exist in the Forest of Dean, with one promontory fort – built around 2,500 years ago – standing a little to the south of the Yat Rock in the parish of English Bicknor. Covering an area of 15 acres, it is protected by a defensive system of five banks and ditches. These ramparts, up to 10 feet in height, were built to protect the southern side of the fort, the other two sides being protected by the steep cliffs of the Wye Gorge. Getting from the car park to the Yat Rock viewpoint involves walking over and

King Arthur's Cave, Great Doward.

The Long Stone, Staunton.

Wibdon Broad Stone, Woolaston.

through the fort, earthen defences clearly visible on either side. An archaeological investigation of 1990–91 revealed fragments of pottery dating back to the first century AD. A model of the fort, showing ramparts and huts, can be seen on a rock near the car park.

Some 14 miles farther south, within a loop of the River Wye, the remains of another promontory fort can be seen at the deserted village of Lancaut. Situated to the north-east of Lancaut Lane, it is protected by sheer cliffs on its north and east sides, with at least two ramparts and ditches along its east side. Offa's Dyke seems to have made use of the fort's defensive ditches during construction, but much of the earthwork is hidden by trees. Lydney Park, around 10 miles to the north-east, is the site of a Romano-British temple and there, too, the promontory on which it stands had been defended in the Iron Age by a hill fort protected by ramparts, which were strengthened by the Romans.

A probable Iron Age site can be seen almost next to the roadside at Soudley, 7 miles to the north-east. Close to a bend in the road near the Dean Heritage Centre, it is partly obscured by rough vegetation and consists of a small enclosed area situated on the end of a ridge, with a defensive bank and outer ditch on the north and west sides. The earthwork occupies the end of a spur and has the appearance of a small Iron Age fort, although the only dating evidence found at the site has been several pieces of Romano-British pottery. It could be that it originated as an Iron Age structure, subsequently being used in the Roman and Norman periods.

Hill fort model, English Bicknor.

Iron Age promontory fort, Lancaut.

A more substantial hill fort is situated within the trees and undergrowth of Welshbury Wood, between Pope's Hill and Abenhall, a few miles farther north. It is thought to date to the Middle Iron Age period from around 300 BC, with features identified from at least the Bronze Age to the beginning of the Roman period. The fort is defended by a single bank and ditch across the north and east sides and a triple rampart on the south and west sides. It is unlikely to have remained in use after the Roman occupation of the Forest of Dean, sometime after AD 50, and a series of charcoal burning platforms are probably connected with the Forest's iron production of the medieval period. Although the site is well preserved, with ramparts up to 5 yards high in places, the climb is not easy and the monument is accessible only to fit and physically mobile enthusiasts.

In addition to these monuments, there has been other evidence of Iron Age activity in the Forest. Curious groups of hollows, subterranean caverns and mossy crags locally known as scowles can be seen at several sites in the district, including the Devil's Chapel, Bream; Stockwood Scowles, Clearwell; Puzzle Wood, Milkwall; and Cudleigh Holes, Upper Soudley. Although scowles were once considered entirely man-made, modern geological research suggests the peculiar fissures and hollows are more likely to be the remains of underground cave systems formed in the limestone rock many millions of years ago. Later uplift and erosion caused exposure of the caves on the surface, with iron ore subsequently forming in the fissures and later being exploited in mining activities. An interesting discovery of an Iron Age coin of the Coriosolites (people from the region now called Brittany) was made at the Devil's Chapel scowle at Bream by a German doctor attached to Coleford's prisoner-of-war camp in the mid-1940s, suggesting pre-Roman exploitation at the site.

Roman Occupation

The Roman occupation of the Forest of Dean was completed sometime after AD 50, following which their exploitation of the area's natural reserves proceeded in earnest, with much evidence of iron smelting having been found throughout the area. Forest of Dean iron ore has been exploited from pre-Roman times, with archaeological research showing that local ores were used to make iron objects from the late prehistoric and Roman periods. In the Coleford area a hoard of over 3,000 Roman coins of the third century AD was found at Milkwall's Puzzle Wood scowles in 1848, suggesting the Romans were actively mining the ore there. They were undoubtedly mining iron ore in the network of caves at nearby Clearwell, too, with the surviving subterranean workings and substantial cave system providing a fascinating visitor attraction.

A fairly large Roman settlement existed at Dymock, on the northern edge of the district, where excavated pottery suggested occupation from the first to the fourth century AD and in 1958 an aerial photograph revealed a Roman road on the eastern side of the village, this being examined when the nearby M50 motorway was under construction. Additionally, foundations and floors of both stone and timber buildings have been excavated. The discovery of possible furnaces and three parallel ditches near the cricket pitch in the 1960s suggested evidence of iron smelting.

DID YOU KNOW?

It is thought by some that Dymock may be the 'lost' Roman town of Macatonion, shown in the eighth century's *Ravenna Cosmography* as located between Gloucester and Kenchester, Herefordshire.

Romano-British sites were identified in 1953 at the small rural settlement of Popes Hill, around 9 miles south of Newent, when evidence of a probable iron-smelting furnace was discovered, pottery finds suggesting occupation from at least the second century to the end of the Roman period. Excavation work carried out at Blakeney, 6 miles south, by the Dean Archaeological Group has revealed evidence of a high-status building – with a heating system and a stoned courtyard – that was constructed around AD 75 and demolished towards the middle of the second century. Situated beside a major Roman military road from Newnham to Caerleon in Monmouthshire, the building was thought to have been an early administration centre for a high-ranking official, possibly appointed to supervise mining and other industrial activities.

At Blackpool Bridge, a little over a mile to the north-west, a good stretch of the ancient Dean Road – which runs from Lydney, to Soudley, Littledean, Abenhall and Mitcheldean – is just about visible alongside the modern-day road. The road, with its kerbing and pitched stone paving, is traditionally supposed to be Roman. Radiocarbon dating carried out in

The ancient Dean Road at Blakeney.

1985, however, found the 8-foot-wide road to be no earlier than seventeenth century. The sample used for the dating process was later shown to be unreliable, however, so it may indeed be that the road is actually Roman. Perhaps 'repairs' and minor reconstructions of the original road have taken place in later centuries.

The southern part of the Forest district was certainly well known to the Romans. A hoard of around 250 Roman coins dated AD 313–46 was discovered at High Woolaston in 1887 and during the 1930s a Roman Villa close to the banks of the River Severn at Woolaston was excavated in a field to the east of Woolaston Grange. The remains, which are now buried in the interests of preservation, indicate it was a large winged-corridor building erected no earlier than AD 300, although the presence of second-century coins and pottery suggested possible earlier occupation on the site. The remains of a small square building at the south-east corner have been interpreted as a lighthouse. Archaeological work between 1987 and 1991 confirmed the presence of a further building and two furnaces to the south-west of the villa. It is likely that significant quantities of iron were produced there, with the probability that it was exported by sea. It may well be that the Romans had a – still to be discovered – harbour nearby.

The Romano-British temple at Lydney Park, a couple of miles to the north-east, is perhaps the Forest of Dean's Roman *pièce de résistance*. Built around AD 365 on a promontory protected by ramparts, and dedicated to the water god Nodens, it was excavated by Mortimer Wheeler in 1928 and again in 1980. The complex consisted of

Roman Temple remains at Lydney Park.

a basilica temple, now reduced to foundations, with a bathhouse and a large building (thought to be a guest house) with ranges of rooms around a central courtyard. It is believed the temple complex may have been more or less abandoned by the end of the fourth century. A number of effigies of dogs, associated with healing cults, were discovered during excavation of the site – one of these Romano-British sculptures is of cast bronze and is of special interest and quality – and these can be seen in Lydney Park museum. The park's gardens and Roman ruins are open to the public on selected days.

In 1982 a second Roman temple site was discovered, this time in the grounds of Dean Hall at Littledean, near Cinderford. The grounds overlook the River Severn and expert opinion suggested the site had been a water shrine venerating Sabrina, the goddess of the River Severn. The hall and its grounds are privately owned, however, and are not open to the public.

DID YOU KNOW?

Rising sea levels of around 5,000 BC submerged a forest near Woolaston, leaving an abundance of stumps and timbers beneath the waters of the Severn Estuary there.

Medieval Period

Following years of confrontations with barbarian tribes in Britain – and facing attacks by barbarians elsewhere in the empire – the Romans left Britain around AD 410 and by the middle of that century the country found itself invaded and settled by waves of Saxons (from northern Germany), Angles (from southern Denmark) and Jutes (from northern Europe). In AD 779 Mercia became the Anglo-Saxon supreme kingdom and Offa, who had come to the throne in AD 757, ruled until his death in AD 796. At some point in his reign – the date is lost to history – he ordered construction of a dyke along the length of the frontier between England and Wales. Sections of Offa's Dyke can be seen in the Forest district, including two short sections near the River Wye at the north-east of English Bicknor parish, as well as a substantial section that runs above the Wye and through a wood called The Fence, to the north-east of Bigsweir Bridge.

The Norman Conquest of Britain in 1066 brought about profound change, of course, and the invaders constructed castles, abbeys and great churches throughout the land – although most of the defensive monuments in the Forest are fairly basic motte-and-bailey constructions.

The Castle Tump at Dymock, on the northern edge of the district, stands beside the B4215 road, and next to Welsh House Lane, around half a mile to the south-east of the village. It was constructed in the eleventh or twelfth century as a timber castle and was, between 1148 and 1154, granted temporarily to William de Braose, by Roger, Earl of Hereford. The large mound of the motte is clearly visible with the flattened area of the bailey surrounding it. It is thought the castle was destroyed by Henry II in the 1150s.

A medieval fortification locally known as Taynton Castle, and thought to date to the eleventh or twelfth century, is visible in Castle Hill Wood, around a mile to the west of Taynton village, around 7 miles south of Dymock. The monument consists of a ringwork castle or motte, which forms an oval enclosure measuring around 30 yards by 25 yards. The rampart bank is around 8 feet wide and 5 to 6 feet high. To the north-east of the village, in fields off Kent's Green Road, there is a site known locally as Swan Tump. This is where Taynton's original medieval church – destroyed during the Civil War – was situated. Additionally, the fields contain a couple of medieval moats and a motte and bailey that are likely to be of the eleventh or twelfth century.

At Ruardean, some 10 miles south-west of Taynton, a manor house stood on a spur to the north-west of the church and was replaced by a castle in the fourteenth century. It was defended by a perimeter wall and is thought to have stood until the early seventeenth century, but by the 1830s little stonework remained and today part of a tower and doorway are all that survive. The castle was reputedly destroyed by Cromwellian troops during the Civil War.

At English Bicknor, around 4 miles south-west, the earthworks of a motte and bailey, with a diameter of 150 yards, are visible in the centre of the village – the village church situated within the outer bailey. It is thought to have perhaps been built around 1140 during the reign of King Stephen, but had been demolished by the late fourteenth century.

Dominated by its Norman castle of 1130, the village of St Briavels, around 8 miles south of English Bicknor, was for centuries the administrative centre of the Forest and was granted a market in 1208, although this had lapsed by around 1700. The castle has a fine gatehouse, which was constructed in 1292–93, and the building is surrounded by a broad

Dymock Castle tump.

Ruardean Castle remains.

moat, denuded of water in the nineteenth century. Although originally used sometimes as a hunting lodge for the king, the castle's main purpose was as the headquarters of the Constable of the Forest. Additionally, it was used as a debtors' prison and as an arsenal for weapons made in the area. Much iron smelting went on at St Briavels – in the thirteenth century there was a forge that belonged to the castle – with numerous orders for armaments and related goods being sent to the Constable. King John ordered 2,000 crossbow quarrels (arrowheads) on one occasion, Henry III is said to have used 6,000 in the year 1223, and in 1333 Edward III ordered 500 pieces of iron for use by his troops. Edward I called it his 'Great Arsenal'. More prosaically, the castle has since 1947 served as a youth hostel.

At Hewelsfield, a couple of miles south-east, a roughly circular mound – thought to be the remains of a medieval motte of the late twelfth or early thirteenth century – is situated a short distance to the south-west of the church. It is a relatively unprepossessing monument, with no evidence of any surviving stonework, and the fort that occupied the site may have been timber.

At Lydney, around 5 miles east and near the River Severn, a site known as Little Camp Hill exists on a hilltop a couple of hundred yards to the south-east of the Romano-British temple complex at Lydney Park. A twelfth-century castle, made up of a keep, gate tower and outer bailey defended by a ditch and bank, stood there until its demolition soon after the end of that century. The surviving earthwork was partially excavated in 1929, revealing the remains of this small stone-built castle, the walls of which are now covered by grass-grown earth banks.

Motte-and-bailey earthworks, English Bicknor.

St Briavels Castle.

Remnants of a Norman castle exist at Newnham, beside the Severn and around 7 miles to the north-east. All that remains visible today is a three-sided grass-covered mound around 5 feet high, with ramparts and a ditch around 15 feet deep. This earthwork forms the remains of a motte and bailey that was more or less levelled by bulldozer in 1957. Excavations in 2012 revealed the foundations of a square, thick-walled building of the twelfth century. This may have been the tower of what was probably a small castle, built to control Newnham and the valley road below. A defensive bank running north is thought to be Civil War earthworks of 1644.

Finally, on a hilltop just over a mile to the north-west, a grass- and tree-covered earthwork known as Littledean Camp is situated to the east of Littledean village. It has a commanding view of the Severn Valley and survives as a Norman motte with a circular bank of stone and earth, and an outer ditch. When excavated in 1958, part of the bank to the west of the entrance was thought to have formed the base for a wooden watchtower. Finds suggested occupation between the late eleventh century and the first half of the twelfth century. The earthwork could be the site of 'the old castle of Dene' mentioned in charters of Henry II in 1153–54, although Welshbury Hill Fort or Taynton Castle could lay equally valid claims to this. The earthwork that remains is in good condition, but is not easily accessible.

Civil War earthworks at Newnham.

2. Civil War Conflict

Although the Forest of Dean did not see any major battles during the Civil War, there were a number of fierce skirmishes and military exchanges. In general, the Forest people did not show great allegiance to either the Royalist or the Parliamentarian side. Gloucester, however, was another matter. It was an important Parliamentarian stronghold in the west of England and its governor, Colonel Edward Massey, conducted several military operations against local Royalists. Edward Somerset, Lord Herbert, at Raglan Castle in Monmouthshire, was determined to put an end to this and assembled an army of 1,500 foot and 500 horse, marching into the Forest on 20 February 1643.

Herbert's first target was Coleford, which was the base of a newly raised regiment of Parliamentarians under Colonel John Berrow. The Royalists had little difficulty in overpowering Berrow's troops and a number of prisoners were taken. The exchange seems to have been short and sharp, the town's market house being torched and many of the defending soldiers scattering in every direction. The Royalists suffered losses,

The Market Place, Coleford.

Former King's Head Hotel, Coleford.

however, with Berrow's men firing on them from the windows of houses. Major-General Sir Richard Lawdley, in command of the foot soldiers, was fatally wounded – according to tradition he was killed by a silver bullet fired from a window in the King's Head Inn. Colonel Jerome Brett took over Lawdley's command, and having prevailed, the Royalists marched on towards Gloucester, halting at Highnam where, on 24 March 1643, they were attacked by a Parliamentarian force. A fierce battle took place, with many of Brett's Welsh soldiers fleeing and subsequently being slaughtered on the banks of the River Leadon at the nearby village of Rudford. A plaque commemorating those who died in the Battle of Coleford has been set into the paving stones of the traffic island at the Market Place.

DID YOU KNOW?

According to tradition a village named Pomerton lies submerged beneath the waters of the River Severn, near Awre. It is mentioned by seventeenth-century topographer, antiquary and Member of Parliament Robert Atkyns (1647–1711) in his county history *The Ancient and Present State of Gloucestershire*. There is no other record of it, however, so whether it actually exists is a matter for conjecture.

Barber's Bridge, Rudford, is at the point where the B4215 road crosses Red Brook, which flows into the River Leadon. Nearby, standing 20 feet high on an embankment beside the road, is a commemorative obelisk, built partly with stones from Gloucester's medieval walls. It was constructed in 1871 to mark the spot where on 24 March 1643 some 500 of the Welshmen fleeing from the battle at Highnam were killed. Large numbers of skeletons had been found in the 1790s during construction of the Herefordshire and Gloucestershire Canal; eighty-six more were revealed in 1868 during work to convert the canal to a railway system; and still more were found during road-widening work in the 1970s. The men were killed on the west bank of the nearby River Leadon where, according to legend, the river ran red with blood. Following the initial discovery of skeletons Barber's Bridge became known locally as Barbarous Bridge.

Some 2.5 miles south of Newent, and just 3 miles west of Rudford, the small village of Taynton is said to have changed allegiance several times during the Civil War. Certainly the medieval Church of St Lawrence was burnt down a few days after the raising of the Siege of Gloucester on 5 September 1643. There seems to be no definitive account of who was responsible. One version has it that the Parliamentarian Colonel Edward Massey occupied the building, storing weapons and ammunition there and eventually being flushed out by a Royalist commander named Captain Wiffin. Another version says Royalists taking refuge there were forced out by the Parliamentarians. But was it Massey or Wiffin who torched the church? What *is* definite, however, is that the church we see today was built in 1650–60 by Thomas Pury, MP for Gloucester during the Civil War and the Long Parliament, with Parliament apparently insisting it should be on a north-south axis rather than the traditional east-west.

Some 6 miles to the south, the church at Westbury, too, was the scene of hostility a few months later. In late January 1644, while it was garrisoned by the Royalists, the occupants were overcome by a Parliamentarian force led by Colonel Massey. The Transactions of the Bristol and Gloucestershire Archaeological Society for 1893–94 state that 'Westbury Church was taken by placing stools and ladders under the windows, from which the attacking party threw hand-grenades into the building, and drove out the enemy.' According to tradition, the nearby Red Lion Inn was used as a hospital for soldiers wounded in the skirmish.

On 7 May 1644 a Royalist garrison at Dean Hall, Littledean, was surprised and defeated by cavalry sent by Colonel Massey. The Roundhead troops stormed the building and captured a group of around twenty soldiers, who went on to break the terms of their surrender and were executed. Two of the officers, Lieutenant-Colonel Congrave and Captain Wigmore, were killed in the dining room at Dean Hall.

A day later, on 8 May 1644, Massey turned his attention to the Royalist garrison at Newnham, beside the River Severn a couple of miles away. The Royalists had fortified the church and the area around the green, but withdrew to the church building as the Parliamentarian soldiers attacked. John Corbett, the Puritan historian of the Siege of Gloucester, states that one of the Royalists, John Tipper, lit a barrel of gunpowder inside the church to blow up the attackers. It exploded, causing men and windows to be blown out of the church, although it appears no one was killed by the explosion. It did, however, succeed in enraging the attacking Parliamentarians and a bloody reprisal followed, with the slaying of around eighteen men.

Barber's Bridge Memorial, Rudford.

The detached tower of Westbury Church.

The village of Redmarley D'Abitot, around 20 miles to the north, is situated at the very edge of the Forest of Dean district. On 2 August 1644 the Battle of Redmarley – in which between 2,000 and 3,000 troops were engaged – took place in fields between Redmarley (at that time in Worcestershire) and the Worcestershire village of Eldersfield, a couple of miles to the east. The Royalist leader, Colonel Mynne – described by Gloucester preacher John Corbet in 1645 as 'a serious and active enemy; a perpetual terror to the countryside' – and his men met with the omnipresent Colonel Massey and his troops, who pushed the Royalists back towards Redmarley village. Conventional military tactics seem not to have been much used and an air of confusion prevailed.

The action moved to the centre of Redmarley as the day progressed, and the Parliamentarians organised a more systematic attack, during which Colonel Mynne was killed, along with 170 of his men. This was the turning point in the battle. The wounded and demoralised Royalists were forced back down Bromsberrow Road, past the village green and on to the village of Donnington, near Ledbury. In trying to get ahead of the fleeing Royalists, Massey came across a Lieutenant-Colonel Passey, who was riding ahead of a Worcester Royalist force of men, intending to support Colonel Mynne's troops. Passey was wounded in the unexpected confrontation, after which Massey and his battle-weary men made haste to the Parliamentarian stronghold of Gloucester. It is not known how many men died in the battle, but it seems almost certain to have been in excess of 200.

Newnham Church.

Just over a month later, in mid-September 1644, Massey was involved in yet more action, this time at Beachley, some 40 miles south-west. Aware of the strategic importance of the Beachley-Aust ferry crossing, Sir John Wintour, Lydney ironmaster and ardent Royalist, and a force of men were digging an extensive trench defence in the vicinity of Offa's Dyke, between the Rivers Wye and Severn, when they were routed by troops under Colonel Massey. Some of the combatants were killed, while others were drowned when they took to the waters of the Severn. Wintour escaped, it is believed, by riding on horseback down the paths of Sedbury Cliffs to a boat waiting on the Severn, while Massey and his men withdrew.

After a pause of around a month, Massey returned on 14 October 1644 to attack the Royalists and their defences. A pitched battle followed, with around thirty Royalists being killed and 220 being taken prisoner. The fight occurred, this time, close to cliffs above the River Wye near Lancaut and Wintour is supposed to have made his escape by jumping off a precipice – still known as 'Wintour's Leap' – into the River Wye 200 feet below. It seems a highly unlikely scenario and it may be that, over the centuries, accounts of Wintour's exploits at Sedbury and at the cliffs near Lancaut derive from a single incident.

In January 1645 Wintour attacked a Parliamentarian garrison at Lydney, overcoming the defences and taking several prisoners. Colonel Massey and a force of men arrived at the scene, however, and succeeded in retaking the garrison. Twenty-six Royalist soldiers were killed in the battle, with a captain and twenty-five men being taken prisoner. Wintour and a force of Royalist troops were a month later encamped at Lancaut, using the place as a base from which to launch raids against Parliamentarian garrisons and

Wintour's Leap.

troop movements, when Massey and his men stormed the defences. Around eighty Royalist soldiers were killed in the attack, with Wintour and some of his men escaping by swimming to a waiting ship.

At the end of March 1645, having overcome the Royalists at Lancaut, Massey sought to harass them further by storming Wintour's heavily fortified mansion at White Cross, on the outskirts of Lydney. The mansion was not overcome, although a number of the defenders were killed in the fighting, but Massey blockaded all of the Royalist garrisons at Lydney and its nearby settlements. On 4 April 1645, however, a large Royalist army – 2000 cavalrymen and more than 500 foot soldiers – under Prince Rupert invaded the Forest. Even the formidable Colonel Massey couldn't counter such a force and the blockade of Wintour's mansion and the surrounding garrisons west of Newnham was relieved. These troops went on, it is said, to abuse the Forest communities and many atrocities were committed upon the inhabitants, who – Prince Rupert claimed – were mostly 'notorious rebels' who had lived under Massey's protection. Unsurprisingly, many of the Forest people hid in the woods and mines, taking arms and whatever they could for subsistence.

After less than a week of plundering, Prince Rupert and his men moved out of the Forest on 9 April 1645 and headed for Herefordshire. Colonel Massey then returned to Lydney to attack the Royalists at White Cross. Wintour, on 8 May 1645, torched his home and property rather than let it fall into Massey's hands and withdrew over the River Wye to Chepstow Castle. He stayed there for only a short time and a few months later his estate was confiscated and awarded to Massey. Wintour's estate was returned to him, however, following the Restoration in 1660.

DID YOU KNOW?

There have been various theories about the origin of the 'Humpty Dumpty' nursery rhyme. In 1956 it was suggested by Professor David Daube that Humpty Dumpty was a siege engine used unsuccessfully in 1643 to try and breach the city walls of Gloucester. Regarded by some academics as credible, the notion was dismissed by others, but has nevertheless achieved a degree of popular acceptance.

3. Significant Buildings and Structures

The Forest of Dean has many noteworthy buildings and structures and a detailed description of them all would fill at least one hefty book. The intention here, then, is to briefly highlight some of the more unusual or frequently overlooked examples.

Situated in the north of the district, and beyond the forested area, Tibberton's Norman church has a particularly grand little Gothic building, with four gables and a central pinnacle, in a corner of the churchyard. This is the Price family mausoleum (William Price was twice MP for Gloucester in the nineteenth century). Hartpury's churchyard, around 4 miles north-east, has a most unusual and curious stone beehive shelter. Constructed around 1840–50, the structure has two tiers of fourteen openings for hives and has a gabled roof with a crested ridge and ball finials. At Upleadon, around 5 miles north-west, the church has a very unusual timber-framed tower, believed to date to around 1500.

Pauntley Court, a couple of miles north, is a half-timbered house – part medieval, part Elizabethan – that belonged to the Whittington family from 1311 until 1545. Richard 'Dick' Whittington, four times Lord Mayor of London, was almost certainly born at the house.

Price Mausoleum, Tibberton.

Beehive Shelter, Hartpury.

Upleadon Church.

In the 1930s Pauntley Court was set up as a 'Home for Wayfarers', but by the 1950s had become a tumbledown farm. Now beautifully restored, the house offers first-class holiday lets in the dovecote and a wing of the main house.

Kempley, 7 miles to the west, possesses two remarkable churches. The tiny Norman Church of St Mary has some of the best-preserved medieval wall paintings in England – although, to the untrained eye, they may be a little hard to properly distinguish. Dating back to the twelfth century, they depict the Last Judgement, Christ seated upon a rainbow, and a number of other fine illustrations. The twelfth-century roof, too, is remarkable, said to be the oldest timber roof of any building in England.

Around a mile south, the early twentieth-century Church of St Edward the Confessor, too, is of considerable interest, being virtually a shrine to the Arts and Crafts movement. Designed by English Arts and Crafts architect, craftsman and inventor Albert Randall Wells, it is a slightly unusual-looking church of local Forest of Dean reddish-brown sandstone. The west window is very large, with a lattice-like diagonal stone grid, and the nave and chancel roofs are steep-pitched, with a strikingly large carving of Christ above the north doorway.

The church at Oxenhall, 3 miles south-east, has a twelfth-century font that is one of only six lead fonts of that date in the county. Newent's church, a mile to the south-east, hasn't had much good fortune in terms of the weather – the original spire was blown down in a great storm in 1662, while the nave was rebuilt after it collapsed following a heavy snowstorm in 1673. Of particular interest in the south porch is part of an Anglo-Saxon cross shaft, thought to date to

Medieval wall painting at the Church of St Mary, Kempley.

The west window of Kempley's Church of St Edward the Confessor.

The twelfth-century font at Oxenhall Church.

the ninth century, upon which there is a depiction of Adam and Eve and a mythical beast. In the Lady Chapel there is an interesting eleventh-century carved stone that was being used as a burial 'pillow stone' when found in 1912, but may have been originally a portable altar.

Some 5 miles to the south, the church at Huntley has a medieval tower, but the rest of the building was demolished and a new church added to the tower in 1862–63. It is a magnificent building that looks as though it must have cost a small fortune to construct, the interior being especially resplendent. The reredos behind the altar has splendidly carved sculptures of the Nativity, the Last Supper, and the Resurrection.

Opposite the church at Longhope, just over 2 miles west, a seventeenth-century timber-framed house named Court Leet was once used as the local courthouse, with the adjacent cottage functioning as the gaol. The village war memorial, too, is interesting, being a sandstone sculpture of a recumbent lion on a stone plinth. It stands in a small paved enclosure and can be seen at the junction of Old Hill and the A4136 road.

With origins in the thirteenth century, the church at Abenhall is around 2.5 miles south-west. A stone shield (renewed in 1982) on the outer western wall of the tower is carved with the arms of the free miners, while inside the building further emblems of Abenhall's free miners and smiths can be seen on the richly carved fifteenth-century font. Additionally, a stained-glass window by Tom Denny, and dedicated in 2011 by the Bishop of Tewkesbury, depicts mining and its links with the church.

A walk of less than half a mile along nearby Lower Spout Lane leads up a path into the woodland, where St Anthony's Well is found. Thought to have been reconstructed in the

The reredos, Huntley Church.

Court Leet, Longhope.

Stone shield bearing the free miners' arms, Abenhall Church.

late eighteenth century, the structure is of large squared stones, with the spring running into a small bathing pool. Twelve stone steps descend to the bath.

First mention of the well came in medieval times, when the monks of nearby Flaxley Abbey, founded around 1150, promoted its links with St Anthony. Prehistoric flint implements and Roman and Iron Age artefacts have been found in the well's vicinity, however, suggesting it may have been a ritual site from early times. The water, believed to contain iron and lime, has long been considered to have healing properties.

The outstanding building at Ruardean, 1.5 miles west, is undoubtedly its twelfth-century church. On the south porch it has a fine tympanum depicting St George and the dragon and, inside, a curious carving of two fishes is set into a wall near the seventeenth-century font. The carving, believed to be a twelfth-century decoration of the south doorway arch, was found in 1956 in the lining of an oven at a nearby cottage, having probably been taken from builder's rubble when the church doorway was built.

The largest building at Cinderford, around 6 miles south-east, is the Baptist Chapel. Built in 1860, it has an impressive stone façade with four Doric columns. The Palace Cinema at nearby Belle Vue Road is a single-storey brick building that had a domed roof for the first few years of its existence. Built in 1911 as an 'Electric or Cinematograph theatre', it is one of the oldest cinemas in the country.

Dean Hall, 1.5 miles south-east at Littledean, has already been mentioned with regard to its Roman and Civil War connections. It is probably of the sixteenth century, although parts of the building may be much older – indeed, it has been claimed as the oldest inhabited house in England.

St Anthony's Well, Mitcheldean.

Twelfth-century tympanum at Ruardean Church.

The subject of numerous 'haunted house' claims, Dean Hall is very much a private residence, and as such, is not open to the public. Fine battlemented gate-piers, with wrought-iron gates dated 1852, can be seen at the entrance to the drive, providing some consolation to the curious.

The well-preserved Littledean Jail, built 1789–91, stands to the north-east of the church. A severe-looking former House of Correction, the prison has a solidly built quadrangular wall that surrounds a two-storeyed central building and four courtyards. A police station from 1854 to 1972, today the building is in private ownership and houses a somewhat macabre crime exhibition.

Flaxley village, a couple of miles north-east, was formerly the site of a Cistercian abbey, which, according to tradition, was founded around 1151 by Roger, Earl of Hereford, to mark the spot where his father had been killed hunting in the Forest of Dean in 1143. In the main, the only parts of the abbey building to survive are sections of the claustral ranges, which have been incorporated into the later manor house called Flaxley Abbey. The abbot's guest chamber in the west range is the main medieval survivor.

Some 2 miles south-east, situated next to the A48 at Westbury-on-Severn, Westbury Court Garden is one of the only surviving seventeenth-century Dutch water gardens in the UK. Features at the garden include tranquil canals, a gazebo of around 1720, lawns and topiaries, yew hedges, shrubs and fruit trees, spring bulbs and a magnificent evergreen oak, believed to be one of the largest and oldest specimens in the country. The garden's Tall Pavilion, built 1702–03, offers an elevated vantage point.

Flaxley Abbey.

Westbury Court Garden.

Speech House, Coleford.

Speech House, often claimed to be at the centre of the Forest, is found on the B4226 road, 7 miles south-west of Westbury. It was built around 1670 as a hunting Lodge for Charles II, as well as a Court of Speech, but was greatly enlarged in 1883. It serves as the administrative centre of the Forest, where important officials known as Verderers meet in the courtroom to administer the laws relating to the Forest of Dean. Originally created to protect the 'vert and venison' – essentially trees, plants and animals – of the Royal Forest, they nowadays meet infrequently, their role being mainly advisory and as an intermediary between the public and the Forestry Commission. The Danish King Canute, King of England from 1016 to 1035, is usually given the credit for establishing the Verderers' Court early in the eleventh century, although some historians have argued that its origin is even earlier.

A small stone obelisk at the roadside opposite the north front of the building marks the traditional centre of the Forest. Probably of the eighteenth century, it was restored in 1957 to mark the fiftieth year of Viscount Bledisloe's service as a Verderer. By around 1840 Speech House was also used as an inn and in 1858 it became a hotel – today the Court Room is the hotel dining room, although it can be viewed by visitors. It retains its original panelled timber ceiling, which was restored in 1956, and it is said that at one time there was a dull red stain upon it. This was claimed to be the blood of a forester who committed suicide while awaiting trial on a poaching charge.

Pillar marking the traditional centre of the Forest.

Rock Castle, Coleford.

Clearwell Castle.

Rock Castle, near the Baptist Chapel at Coleford, 3 miles to the south-west, is a curious folly of around 1850. A square pink and white building with a rounded corner tower, it is a roughcast sham castle with pointed windows, which some have suggested may have been designed by Henry Poole, Vicar of Coleford from 1818.

Clearwell, just over 2 miles south-west, has several buildings of note. Its opulent church, constructed of local red sandstone in 1863–64, has a tall steeple and a sumptuous interior that features a striking mixture of blue, red and white stone. French Gothic in style, there is much brass, stained glass and elaborate carving, with the reredos screen at the back of the altar being especially noteworthy.

Clearwell Castle, a short distance to the south of the church, may at first glance appear to be a genuine medieval castle, but is actually a rather handsome neo-Gothic stone folly that was built in 1727–28. It was badly damaged by fire in 1930, became vandalised and narrowly escaped demolition, until in 1952 it was bought by the son of a former gardener on the estate, who gradually restored it. It is now a hotel and wedding venue.

Newland, 1.5 miles north-west, possesses an exceptionally large church for such a small village. Construction of the church, which is widely known in the district as the 'Cathedral of the Forest', began in the early thirteenth century, although most of the building seen today is of the late thirteenth or early fourteenth century.

The 'Cathedral of the Forest' at Newland.

Miner's Brass, Newland
Church.

DID YOU KNOW?

Clearwell Castle was used as a recording location by several rock bands, including Badfinger and Sweet, in the 1970s. In 1973 Black Sabbath rented the castle while working on material for what would become the *Sabbath Bloody Sabbath* album, with guitarist Tony Iommi forming the iconic riff for the song 'Sabbath Bloody Sabbath' while working in the dungeon there.

Newland's church has a number of interesting features, including a good collection of medieval monuments, although many visitors call especially to see the unique 'Miner's Brass' in the south chapel. A rectangular brass, 1 foot in length, it displays a Forest of Dean miner dressed in working garb – pick in hand, hod on his back and candleholder clenched in his teeth. Its origins are unknown, but it is said to be of the fifteenth century, having been 'returned to the church' in the early nineteenth century. Running along the south side of the churchyard are some attractive almshouses of 1617.

Bigsweir Bridge, between Monmouth and Chepstow, was built in 1827 and crosses the River Wye at a point 5 miles south-west of Newland. Straddling the English and Welsh border, it carries the A466 road between the Parishes of St Briavels in Gloucestershire and Llandogo in Monmouthshire. Graceful and aesthetically pleasing, the bridge is a cast-iron construction, comprising a single arch of 164 feet, with spandrel bracing, cast-iron balustrade and stone abutments.

At Brockweir, 3 miles south of Bigsweir Bridge, another substantial iron bridge, supported by two pairs of solid iron columns, crosses the River Wye. Nearby, on the banks of the river, is a rendered white Moravian Church. The ancient Norman church at Hewelsfield, 2.5 miles east, is mainly of the twelfth to thirteenth century, although its roughly circular churchyard – with a yew said to date to around AD 700 – suggests the site may be pre-Christian.

Named after St Cewydd, a sixth-century Welsh saint, Lancaut is a deserted village within a bend of the River Wye, around 6 miles south of Brockweir. Very little now remains above ground, except the crumbling ruins of the twelfth-century Church of St James on a promontory above the nearby river. Abandoned around 1865, now only the

Brockweir's iron bridge and quay.

The ancient church and graveyard at Hewelsfield.

The Moravian Church, Brockweir.

roofless nave and chancel survive, with a double bellcote beneath the west gable. Fine views of the limestone cliffs alongside the Wye can be enjoyed from the church, with the spectacular Wynd Cliff standing on the Welsh side of the river.

Tutshill, 2 miles south-east of Lancaut, is very close to the border with Wales. The border actually runs through the middle of the River Wye and the three bridges linking England and Wales. The bridge carrying the A48 road was built in 1988 and runs immediately parallel to Brunel's railway bridge of 1849–52, while John Rastrick's elegant iron road bridge of 1816 – with five arches resting on huge piers – carries local traffic from Chepstow to Tutshill. From this bridge there are impressive views of the sheer limestone riverside cliffs downstream.

A curious old and dilapidated stone tower of uncertain origin and purpose stands in a garden at Mopla Road, at the northern edge of Tutshill. It overlooks the River Wye and has been suggested as a lookout tower or even a windmill – a windmill was recorded on the site in 1584 and is said to have been rebuilt as a folly in 1815. It has been claimed, too, as the remnant of a sixteenth-century beacon tower, although this seems entirely conjectural. Although situated on private property, it can be seen from the nearby Offa's Dyke path.

A couple of miles south of Tutshill, the ruins of an ancient chapel, abandoned in the 1540s, are just visible in the Severn Estuary around half a mile south-west of Beachley.

The ruined church, Lancaut.

Rastrick's iron bridge, linking England and Wales.

The ruined tower at Tutshill.

Overlooked by the Severn Bridge, it stands on a tiny island called Chapel Rock – barely accessible even at low tide – and comprises a few walls and an archway dating back to the thirteenth century. St Tecla was, according to legend, a fourth- to fifth-century princess from north Wales who went to live a life of religious abstinence on Chapel Rock. Murdered by Saxon raiders, she was subsequently martyred as Saint Tecla of Gwynedd. The rock can be accessed by the intrepid using a track that passes Beachley Lifeboat Station and beneath the Severn Bridge.

At Woolaston, 5 miles north-east, a bridge that crosses the Cone Brooke between Alvington and Woolaston – and accessed by footpaths from Station Road, Woolaston or Church Lane, Alvington – is of particular interest, being the only bridge of its kind in the Forest of Dean. The ancient Mickla Bridge is a double-clapper footbridge, constructed from four very large stone slabs that rest on stone abutments and a central pillar. It was once used by packhorses, but is not thought earlier than fourteenth century and is first mentioned as a footbridge in 1681.

Finally, at Naas Lane, a little way to the north of Lydney harbour, the impressive Jacobean Naas House is a handsome stone building with parapeted gables, mullioned windows, tall chimneys and a central turret with a lead-covered cupola. Although not particularly well known, it is one of the finest houses in the area.

Chapel Rock, Beachley.

Mickla Bridge, Woolaston.

Naas House, Lydney.

4. Industry

Exploitation of the Forest of Dean's natural reserves has taken place since ancient times. There is evidence that iron ore mining occurred since at least the Iron Age, and the Romans certainly carried out iron smelting at a number of locations in the area. Stone has been quarried throughout the Forest for centuries and timber was much used in connection with charcoal burning, as well as for boatbuilding at settlements near the River Severn and River Wye. Running through the highest ground in the Forest are a number of coal seams, one of these, known as the Coleford High Delf seam, being by far the most productive, sustaining numerous collieries through the eighteenth and nineteenth centuries. The last of the big pits closed in 1965, however, and today only a very small number of relatively small-scale pits remain in operation. Commencing in the north of the district, locations where visible traces of former industrial activity remain are described below.

Coal mining to a very limited degree has occurred at Newent on the northern edge of the Forest of Dean district. Some disused shafts at Hawthorne Hill, to the west of Oxenhall, form the remnants of Newent Colliery, which existed from around 1876 to 1880.

Former blowing engine house of Newent Ironworks.

Tower of the Euroclydon building, Drybrook.

It was never profitable, however, and soon became disused. Newent's ironworks, which operated from around 1639 until at least 1751, was a more successful operation and a few of its surviving features are visible at Furnace Lane. A large seventeenth-century sandstone barn with substantial buttresses is part of Furnace Farm and was the charcoal store for the ironworks. Nearby, slightly to the south, is a small gabled building of brick on a high stone plinth, which was the blowing house.

Mitcheldean, around 8 miles to the south-west, was a productive iron-working centre from the thirteenth to sixteenth century, and in the nineteenth century much quarrying was carried out in the parish. The Fairplay Iron Mine opened in 1856 at Plump Hill and operated until around 1907 when its mine machinery was sold. The mine's well-preserved engine house survives at the northern edge of Haywood Plantation, near the A4136 road and around half a mile to the west of Fairplay Cottages.

Hopes of wealth were raised at Mitcheldean when in 1906 a gold mine was opened at Lea Bailey, on Wigpool Common. Gold was indeed discovered, but in such miniscule quantities that extraction was not commercially viable and the mine closed. In 1921 the mine was extended and used for the extraction of iron ore, but was abandoned after a few years. In 2013, however, the Lea Bailey Light Railway Society was formed and work to restore a narrow-gauge line into the mine gathered pace. The former mine can be reached from the Hawthorns Road, to the north of Drybrook.

A somewhat ostentatious example of the wealth some gained from mining exploits can be seen on a hill a little to the north of Drybrook. A large classically styled house known as Euroclydon, which was built around 1860 by colliery owner T. B. Brain, overlooks the village and has a five-stage battlemented tower on its south side. Added in 1876, this imposing and curious-looking tower has a wrought-iron balcony with a view north into Herefordshire.

Several nature reserves in the Forest are good examples of how former industrial sites can return to the wild in a fairly short time. On the northern side of the A4136 road,

Fairplay Iron Mine engine house, Mitcheldean.

The former Lea Bailey Gold Mine, Mitcheldean.

Plump Hill Dolomite Quarry, Mitcheldean.

and around a mile south of Mitcheldean, the Plump Hill Dolomite Quarry Reserve was an active quarry in the late nineteenth and early twentieth centuries, the workings principally being used for road metal and kiln lime. Sadly, it was the scene of a tragic industrial accident in 1872, when four quarry workers died when overcome by poisonous fumes from gunpowder used to shatter a rock face. Today, though, it is a picturesque site, with splendid views across the Severn Vale to the Cotswolds. The quarry has three steep rock faces that, with the quarry floor, have been colonised by plant species and wildlife.

The important remains of a seventeenth-century blast furnace, said to have been built by Lydney ironmaster and ardent Royalist Sir John Wintour, can be found near the start of Lower Spout Lane, at an area called Shapridge, which is to the south of Abenhall village, around a mile south of Mitcheldean. It operated from 1629, being used in the production of armaments – many of which fell into the hands of Cromwell's supporters. In 1650 Parliament ordered the furnace's destruction, but it was rebuilt in 1683 and remained in use until it was converted to a paper mill in 1738. Much of its original form remains more or less complete, however, with a blowing arch and wheel-pit on its west side. It is thought to be named after William Gunn, the owner or occupier of the mill site in 1620. When visited in 2018, however, the furnace was entirely swathed in scaffolding and a protective covering and was clearly the subject of a major restoration project.

The small village of Ruardean is situated on a hillside around 3 miles west of Mitcheldean, and enjoys fine views across the Wye Valley towards the Black Mountains of South Wales. In the 1790s coal seams were being exploited near Ruardean Woodside and Ruardean Hill, the highest point in the Forest of Dean. The site of the former Woodside Colliery is at Pan Tod beacon on the summit, where there is a topograph and sculpture of a crouching miner, unveiled in 2008 as a memorial to five Ruardean Hill colliers who lost their lives working in the mines. A nearby monument of steel and stone, which records the names of fifty Forest of Dean men who died in mining accidents, was unveiled in 2017. The principal coal mines during Ruardean's industrial period were Ruardean Hill Pit, True Blue Pit and Woodside Colliery. The main coal mines had closed by the 1950s, although opencast mining continued until the 1980s.

Two Ruardean-born brothers, James and William Horlick, were in the 1860s responsible for beginning the development of the famous Horlicks malt drink. This originally took place in a shed that stands behind The Malt Shovel public house in the village High Street. In 1887 the Horlick brothers, by this time living near Chicago in the USA, trademarked the name 'malted milk'. James Horlick subsequently returned to England to promote his American-made drink and was later made a baronet.

Brierley is just under 2 miles south of Ruardean. Among the trees of Serridge Inclosure, to the south of the A4136 road through the village, there are disused shafts and a few scant remnants of the Strip-and-at-it Colliery, which operated from at least the mid-nineteenth century and was active until the 1920s.

A furnace at Cinderford Ironworks, around 3 miles south-east of Brierley, operated from 1795 until 1894. Coal mining, however, was Cinderford's main industry through the nineteenth and twentieth centuries. There were hundreds of mines in the forest, and though many of them were small pits or levels that produced only modest amounts of coal, there were some larger, deeper collieries. Waterloo Colliery at Lydbrook, which

Miners' Memorial at Pan Tod Beacon, Ruardean.

The Horlicks building, Ruardean.

opened in 1815, was a deep and productive mine that operated until its closure in 1959. In 1949 a potentially catastrophic incident occurred there when the pit began rapidly filling with floodwater. Although several pit ponies were drowned, no miners were lost – thanks to the actions of mining hero Harry Toomer of Ruardean Woodside, whose expert knowledge of the mine enabled him to lead 177 fellow miners to safety. He subsequently received the British Empire Medal from King George VI in recognition of his actions.

Limekilns were common features in the Forest during the eighteenth and nineteenth centuries. Obtained by heating limestone at very high temperature, the lime was used as a fertiliser in agriculture, a type of cement and as a paint for waterproofing walls. A group of four restored tunnel-vaulted limekilns of the early nineteenth century can be seen just above The Royal Spring Inn, at Vention Lane on the east side of Lydbrook, around 4 miles north-west of Cinderford.

Among several relatively small collieries, the Lightmoor and Northern United collieries at Cinderford were deep mines that produced significant quantities of coal. Coal was first struck at Lightmoor in 1846, and over the following years it became one of the most productive coal mines in the Forest, with just short of 600 men being employed underground by the end of the nineteenth century. Mining in the forest had always been hampered by the presence of water underground, however, due to geological faults and the nature of the strata. In the 1930s there was a slump in the demand for coal, and in

Limekilns, Lydbrook.

Monument to the Forest of Dean miners, Cinderford.

1940, when the coal seam had become exhausted, the colliery was closed. To the south of Cinderford, the former colliery site can be seen in the Lightmoor Inclosure, off Speech House Road (south) and close to the course of the disused Severn and Wye Railway line. Today it is a timber yard, but a curious three-storey stone building – formerly the colliery's engine house, built around 1840–50 – remains there. The former railway line, now an excellent path and cycle-way, passes this structure and timber yard, which is fenced off but affords a good view of the engine house.

Trafalgar Colliery was situated in Serridge Inclosure, to the east of the town and close to Brierley's Strip-and-at-it Colliery. It is believed that work began on the mine around 1860 and, by 1880 there were two shafts being worked by some 600 men below ground, producing 700 tons of coal each day. As at other mines, however, the influx of water was a serious issue and the colliery closed in 1925.

The third and last deep mine at Cinderford was called Northern United. It opened in 1933 and was situated to the north-west of the town, on the northern edge of Birch Wood. Thirty years later, however, large-scale coal mining in the Forest of Dean was no longer considered economically viable and Northern United was closed on Christmas Day 1965. A total of 1,120 tons of coal had been raised in the week preceding the mine's closure. Much of the area has been landscaped, but a few remnants of the colliery survive, including the brick pithead baths. Probably of more interest, however, is a miners' memorial sculpture at the site of the colliery's shaft. Intended to evoke a sense of the deep

Lightmoor Colliery engine house, Cinderford.

Woorgreens Lake, Cinderford.

mine shaft, it consists of a steel tower with a small carved group of miners set within the shaft, as though descending in the cage. Eight miners lost their lives at the Northern United colliery during the time of its existence. The colliery site is reached by following a track for a short distance to the south of the A4136 road between Nailbridge and Brierley. Close to the entrance of what is clearly some sort of industrial site, a notice directs one to follow a series of white posts through the ferns and brambles for a short distance to the monument. Back in the centre of Cinderford town, however, in an area called The Triangle, a statue of a miner stands as a tribute to the miners of the Forest of Dean.

The Woorgreens Nature Reserve, found in woodland a little north of the B4226 between Cinderford and Speech House, is another of the Forest's former industrial sites that has gone on to provide habitat for a variety of wildlife and plant life. Developed after opencast mine working ceased at the site in 1981, it comprises a lake, marsh and heath maintained by the Gloucestershire Wildlife Trust.

Northern United Mine Memorial, Cinderford.

Findall Chimney, Upper Soudley.

Littledean, a mile south-east of Cinderford, was a centre of ironworking in the thirteenth century and at Flaxley, a couple of miles north-east, ironworking flourished into the nineteenth century. Westbury Brook Iron Mine opened there in 1837, and by the time it closed in 1893, almost a million tons of iron ore had been produced. The former mine is now a caving site accessible only to experienced cavers.

The hamlet of Broadoak, beside the River Severn and around 2 miles south of Flaxley, had a small shipbuilding industry and some river trade in the eighteenth century, although this was more significant at nearby Newnham, which became an important transhipment point for the Forest of Dean, with coal, timber and hides being taken along the Severn to Bristol and other destinations. The scant remains of Newnham Quay, which was in existence from at least 1775, are to be seen close to the northern end of Church Road.

At Bullo Pill, just over a mile south of Newnham, various goods were shipped from the harbour and wharf, particularly in the later years of the nineteenth century, and a small industrial centre grew up around the dock. Trade declined, though, with the last official transhipment occurring in 1928. Thereafter, Bullo Pill's condition progressively deteriorated, with the silted-up harbour and a few derelict vessels being melancholy reminders of its once-busy past. In 1991, however, new lock gates were installed and the dock was cleared of silt. Some private boats are now stored and refurbished there, although activity is very limited.

Coal mining was a major source of employment at the Forest villages of Yorkley, Pillowell, Whitecroft and Bream, but the area's coal industry declined after the 1930s and most of the collieries had closed by the mid-1960s, in many cases leaving little sign of their former existence. Parkend, around 3 miles north of Lydney and around 4 miles south-east of Coleford, was once the Forest's industrial heartland.

Former blowing engine house of Parkend Ironworks.

Bullo Pill.

The former quay at Newnham.

A coke-fired furnace called Parkend Ironworks was constructed a little north of the railway station in 1799, and by 1840 up to 70 tons of iron per week were being made. Trade subsequently slumped, however, and in 1877 the works were closed. Most of the associated buildings were demolished, but the blowing engine house survived and today houses the Dean Field Studies Centre, owned and operated by Bristol City Council. Although not open to the general public, this fine building can be seen from New Road in the centre of the village.

Parkend became a centre for coal mining from the eighteenth century, and by the late nineteenth century most of the Forest's main collieries were near Cinderford or Parkend. Jupiter Colliery, New Fancy Colliery, Harmony Colliery, Catch Can Colliery, As You Like It Pit and Parkend Main Colliery were just a few of the many coal-mining enterprises sited in and around the village. Sinking of shafts at the New Fancy Colliery began around 1852, some 500 tons of coal being produced per day in 1906, and it became one of the largest and most productive coal mines in the area. Coal reserves became depleted, however, and the colliery closed in 1944.

The site of the former colliery is now a Forestry Commission amenity site and, with the innovative input of the Forest of Dean Local History Society, has become a popular and informative tourist destination. It is to be found a little over a mile to the north-east of Parkend village, off Fancy Road and along the minor road to Speech House. A striking 'Roll of Honour' sculpture to honour those killed or injured in the mines and quarries of the Forest was unveiled at the site in 2005. A second feature of considerable interest can be seen near the sculpture. This is a geomap that illustrates both the geological landscape and the industrial history of the Forest of Dean, with each of the Forest's coal mines, iron mines, stone quarries, railways and tramways represented by metal discs indicating each location.

The Miners' Memorial, Parkend.

Hod Boy sculpture, Upper Soudley.

Blue Rock Trail and 'Nearly There' statue, Upper Soudley.

A former mill at Lower Soudley, some 5 miles to the north-east, houses the Dean Heritage Centre, in which there is a museum telling the history of the Forest of Dean and displaying a number of interesting artefacts, including an 1830s beam engine from Cinderford's former Lightmoor Colliery.

Commencing at the Heritage Centre or from an old railway cutting at Upper Soudley's Top Road, the 'Blue Rock Trail' follows a gravelled walk of 3 miles that takes in several disused quarries where geological formations created over many millions of years can be seen. Other interesting features along the trail include a sculpture commemorating the young 'Hod boys' once employed to haul hods or boxes of coal from the coalface for onward transportation, a memorial stone to the 5,000 Forest sheep culled in the 2001 foot-and-mouth outbreak, and a statue entitled *Nearly There*. Towards the end of the trail a particularly interesting ventilation furnace and chimney of the former Findall Iron Mine is found to the north of a series of scowle depressions called Cudleigh Holes. Constructed of sandstone around 1800, with a fireplace at its base, it stands to a height of around 15 yards. A fire would be lit and the fumes would rise up the chimney, causing fresh air to be drawn into the mine workings along a masonry flue, thereby preventing the accumulation of carbon dioxide. Extensively restored in the 1970s, it is the only almost-complete iron mine chimney surviving in the forest.

Around 2 miles north of Parkend, Cannop Ponds consist of two large ponds that were artificially created in the nineteenth century to provide water to power a very large waterwheel at Parkend Ironworks, to the south. Fed by a leat off Cannop Brook, the lower

Dean Heritage Centre, Soudley.

Cannop Ponds.

Union Colliery memorial stone, Bixslade.

pond was created in 1825, the upper pond being added in 1829 when the water supply was found inadequate. Even with this additional pond, the water supply was never particularly effective and the ironworks closed in 1877, with the ponds remaining as a tranquil tourist attraction.

An interesting and poignant curiosity can be seen at Bixslade, less than half a mile from the B4234 road near the southern end of Cannop Ponds, and close to Mine Train Quarry and Monument Mine (one of only a handful of mines still producing coal in the Forest). This is a stone memorial to men who died in the Union Colliery disaster of 1902, when a shaft where miners were working became flooded. Although a number of men escaped to safety, four miners were drowned, two of the victims being brothers whose bodies were found in an upright position and hand in hand. The mining disaster is one of the worst to hit the Forest of Dean coalfield.

Cannop Cycle Centre in the Cannop Valley can be found next to the B4234 road between Parkend and Lydbrook, just over a mile north of Cannop Ponds. Standing on the former site of Cannop Colliery, which closed in 1960, it is the starting point for several forest cycle trails – one of which runs along the former Severn and Wye Railway line, taking in the former station sites at Drybrook Road, Cannop Wharf and Speech House Road, as well as remnants of the former Foxes Bridge, Lightmoor and New Fancy collieries.

When following the B4234 road from the Cycle Centre towards Lydbrook for around half a mile, one arrives at the Forestry Commission's Speculation Car Park. From this point there is a Forest of Dean Local History Society 'mines trail', which takes in the sites of some fifteen former collieries over a distance of 6.5 miles, although in most cases there is little to see except some old tips, filled-in shafts and stone foundations. Excellent leaflets detailing this and other trails can be obtained at various outlets in the area and online at www.forestofdeanhistory.org.uk.

Hopewell Colliery Museum and Working Mine can be found at Speech House Road, Coleford. Opened in 1823, it is still a working mine throughout the winter and operates as a museum in the summer months, offering underground tours, guided by an experienced free miner.

In the 1790s two furnaces were built at Whitecliff, on Coleford's Newland Road, and for a short time noted metallurgist David Mushet was involved with production. The forges were unprofitable, however, and he withdrew, with the furnaces being abandoned by around 1812. The surviving ruins, which can be seen from the roadside, are of considerable importance to industrial archaeologists and those with an interest in the area's history.

The ancient and enigmatic Puzzle Wood at Milkwall, around a mile south-east of Coleford, is a 14-acre site containing the curious geological features known locally as scowles – described earlier. A hoard of over 3,000 third-century AD Roman coins found at the wood in 1848 suggests the Romans were actively exploiting the iron ore found within the rocks there. A maze of paths was laid down in the early nineteenth century, creating access to the wood and enabling picturesque walks to be taken among the mossy rocks and gnarled trees.

Hopewell Colliery entrance, Coleford.

Remains of the furnace at Whitecliff Ironworks, Coleford.

Iron ore mines were opened up at the village in the 1820s and a deep iron ore mine named Easter Mine was worked from 1846, employing around fifty men and boys, but production ceased in 1924. The most important industrial site in Milkwall, however, is the former Dark Hill Ironworks, situated at Gorsty Knoll to the east of the village and accessible from a nearby Forestry Commission car park. A purpose-built viewing platform provides a good overview of the site.

Noted Scottish metallurgist David Mushet began work at the site in 1818, building a coke-fired 'experimental furnace', with much of the ironworks being used for research and experiments. Soon after his retirement in 1845, however, the furnace ceased operating. In 1862, one of his sons, Robert Mushet, began a new enterprise immediately adjacent to the ironworks. The Titanic Steelworks employed 300 men, but the business was ultimately unprofitable and Mushet concentrated on experimental work, in 1868 inventing 'R. Mushet's Special Steel'. The Titanic Steelworks closed down in 1871. The ruins seen today include the walls of the blast furnace and blowing engine house among many other remains, including brickworks, kiln bases and storage areas. The site is certainly among the most important industrial archaeological sites in the Forest of Dean.

The village of Clearwell, around 2 miles south-west of Milkwall, is at the edge of the Forest and only a couple of miles from the River Wye. Its well-known caves comprise a natural system of passages that form relics of underground iron ore mining, more than half a million tons of iron ore having been extracted between 1832 and 1880. The last commercial raising of iron ore took place in 1945. Nine large caverns are today open to the public, providing an impressive insight into the scale of mining that took place at Clearwell.

Redbrook is around 3 miles west of Clearwell. A blast furnace and foundry operated near Swan Pool beside the road to Newland from 1604, with a second furnace further down towards the River Wye. These operated until around 1816; other enterprises included a copper works, and a tinplate factory that closed in 1961. Water from Swan Pool fed reservoir ponds that supported these industries.

The hamlet of Brockweir, on the River Wye 8 miles to the south, was once a major boatbuilding centre, with vessels of up to 500 tons being built at sites close to the river. Brockweir Quay was, from at least the seventeenth century, an important transhipment point for Forest goods. It was restored in 2009.

Remains of Dark Hill Ironworks, Milkwall.

Blacksmith's foundry, Clearwell Caves.

Swan Pools, Redbrook.

5. Canals and Railways

Canals

Of the four canals that were situated either wholly or partly in the Forest of Dean, only one – the Hereford and Gloucester Canal – was more than a couple of miles long. It opened from Over (just outside Gloucester) to the northern edge of Newent in 1795, and on to the nearby village of Oxenhall, where from 1792 to 1798 a tunnel of 2,192 yards was constructed. The canal did not reach Hereford until 1845, however, and – the cost and effort of building the tunnel having proved ruinous to the company – it closed in 1881. The tunnel is situated on privately owned farmland, however, and is unfortunately not easily accessible.

A well-restored section of the canal is situated to the north-east of Oxenhall Church, where, south of Coldharbour Bridge (near Brook Cottage), the waterway runs to Oxenhall House Lock. A brick lock-keeper's cottage of 1838 stands close to the lock-side. Large ponds to the east of the church were constructed to provide water for the ironworks that existed a little to the south, at Newent's Furnace Lane, in the seventeenth century.

Cinderford Ironworks, situated in the valley to the west of Cinderford town – around 12 miles south-west of Newent – was a coke-fired blast furnace that was constructed in 1795. Coal was brought to the ironworks along a private canal, specially constructed for

Restored lock and canal section, Oxenhall.

the purpose, which ran for a mile and a quarter from a dam pool at Broadmoor. The ironworks closed in 1894 and had been demolished by 1901. The town's Valley Road follows the route of Cinderford Canal to the site of the ironworks, but today virtually nothing remains of either the canal or ironworks, with only clinker deposits providing evidence of the former blast furnace activity.

Both of the Forest's other canals are situated at Lydney, some 9 miles south. A very narrow strip of water that ran alongside the town's Newerne Stream before connecting with the River Lyd was once known as Pidcock's Canal. It was constructed from 1778 to serve forges operated by the Bathurst family, with another canal, Lydney Canal, opening in 1813 and leading to Lydney Harbour. It connected to Pidcock's Canal and ran for a distance of 1 mile, while Pidcock's Canal ran for a further mile and a half, becoming disused after 1840.

Lydney's outer harbour had been completed in 1821, with the north pier being extended in 1825. Both the harbour and canal remained busy waterways and transhipment points for many years until, after some years of inactivity, the harbour closed in 1977. The canal, however, remained in commercial use until the 1980s. Today it is a peaceful and charming historical relic, populated by pleasure sailing craft. The swing bridge at the canal entrance is a listed structure.

Lydney Canal.

The swing bridge between the harbour and canal, Lydney.

The harbour mouth, Lydney.

DID YOU KNOW?

Wild boar became extinct in the Forest of Dean in the sixteenth or seventeenth century, but significant numbers have colonised the area again, following escapes and illegal releases of farm-reared boar in the 1990s and in 2004. The animals frequently damage amenity grasslands in their search for nutrients and in 2016 the press reported that 'rampaging' animals had broken into Parkend churchyard and 'desecrated' several graves there. In searching for nutrients the boar had rooted up areas of grass and turf, but fortunately stopped short of digging up burials or damaging memorials.

Tramroads and Railways

From the late 1700s the Forest of Dean has been criss-crossed by a network of tramroads and railways, although the majority of these closed in the 1960s, or earlier. Only two lines now exist: the section of the Great Western Railway line that runs alongside the River Severn between Gloucester and Chepstow, situated on edge of the district; and the Dean Forest Railway, a heritage line that runs between Lydney and Parkend on the former Severn and Wye Railway. The impact of the railways on the district was substantial, with buildings, bridges, tunnels and embankments being the obvious physical signs. Many buildings and structures have long been demolished, although a number of interesting remnants survive. Some of the more accessible sites are described below.

The Hereford and Gloucester Canal, which ran past the northern edge of Newent, closed in 1881 and its conversion to a railway line began, with the Ledbury and Gloucester Railway and Newent Railway station opening in 1885. The line subsequently closed in 1964, with the buttresses of the Station Bridge surviving at the junction of Old Station Road and Bridge Street.

As an important centre for industry for hundreds of years, Lydbrook, around 13 miles to the south-west, was served by the Forest's railway network until the mid-1960s. Lydbrook Junction station, on the Ross and Monmouth Railway, opened in 1873 and the old railway bridge that carried the line across the River Wye and on to Ross still stands, despite the line's closure in 1964. Earlier there had been two other stations in the village, as well as an impressively high viaduct, which was constructed of iron and stood on stone piers, but was dismantled in 1965. Very little trace of the former railway infrastructure exists today, except the viaduct abutments and, of course, the bridge across the River Wye. The bridge was in 2018 swathed with scaffolding as major repair work took place.

Authorised in 1870, the Severn and Wye Railway's Lydbrook branch opened for goods traffic in 1874. It ran through Serridge Inclosure to the west of Brierley, under Mierystock Bridge and through Mierystock Tunnel (which passes beneath the A4136 road), before descending to Lydbrook. Work on the 242-yard tunnel had started in 1872. Passenger services on the line ceased in 1929 and in 1956 goods traffic was closed from Mierystock to Lydbrook. The line finally closed in 1960. In 2007, the bridge and tunnel – which had

Mierystock Bridge, Brierley.

Mierystock Tunnel, Brierley.

been blocked with earth for years – were opened again, following a £50,000 grant from ITV's 'People's Millions' and Big Lottery Fund partnership. The entire site is, however, relatively overgrown again, although a view of both bridge and tunnel mouth is available from a path off the A4136 road, near its junction with the B4234.

A fine mid-Victorian railway bridge can be seen at Cinderford, some 5 miles to the south-east. Built around 1870, it stands close to the Dilke Memorial Hospital and carries the B4226 Speech House Road over the former Severn and Wye Railway – now an excellent path and cycle-way.

In 1814 a horse-drawn mineral tramway was completed that ran east from Cinderford bridge to a dock at Bullo Pill, on the banks of the River Severn around 5 miles south-east. In 1900 a railway station was opened at Valley Road, although it closed in 1966. Today the station site has been covered by a housing development called 'The Keelings', named after the railway engineers who brought the railway to Cinderford.

The construction of the tramway to Bullo Pill involved the driving of a tunnel some 1,083 yards in length under Haie Hill. This was the longest railway tunnel in the world at the time of its construction in 1810. The line, which had become part of the Forest of Dean Railway in 1826, was taken over by the South Wales Railway in 1851 and, in 1854, the Great Western Railway subsequently rebuilt the line in broad gauge, which involved

Dilke Railway Bridge, Cinderford.

Derelict signal box, Awre.

Purton Viaduct.

enlargement of the tunnel at Haie Hill. This was carried out by the great Isambard Kingdom Brunel, who described it as 'the most difficult task I have yet undertaken'. At the completion of the work the tunnel had become shorter, losing 19 yards at its east end. Both portals of the tunnel, which is not easily accessible, are bricked up.

Situated around a mile south-west of Awre village, which is a couple of miles south-east of Bullo Pill, a station known as Awre for Blakeney, or sometimes simply Awre Junction, opened in 1851 with the South Wales line from Gloucester to Chepstow. It became a junction when the Forest of Dean Central Railway, a single track created to serve the collieries in the heart of the forest, opened in 1868. The station was situated just south of a level crossing over the Blakeney to Awre road. The actual junction of the two lines was to the north of the level crossing, a brick signal box of 1909 standing between the lines. Awre station closed to passengers in 1959, but the signal box remained in use until 1973. No trace of the station remains, but the derelict shell of the signal box can still be seen.

Around 5 miles south-west of Awre, the tiny hamlet of Purton sits beside the River Severn. Just to the north, and on the edge of Purton Wood, a three-arched viaduct of considerable industrial archaeological interest can be seen crossing the Purton to Etloe Lane. It was built around 1830, forming part of the early stages of the proposed Purton Steam Carriage Road. Proposed in 1826, this was intended to be a tramway linking the River Severn at Purton, via Blakeney, to the collieries in the heart of the Forest. Construction had begun rather prematurely, though, and the parliamentary bill to enable the scheme failed in 1832. As a result, work was stopped and the infrastructure was never used.

Blakeney is around 2 miles north of Purton. Several arches of the ten-span sandstone viaduct that formerly carried the Forest of Dean Central Railway's mineral line from

Blackpool Bridge, Blakeney.

Blakeney Viaduct.

Forest collieries to the junction at Awre can be seen near the junction of New Road and Clark's Lane. The line opened in 1868, but was never commercially successful and traffic ceased in 1949, although official closure was not announced until 1959. Blackpool Bridge, which carried the line over the Soudley road around a mile to the north-west of the village, can be seen near the ancient Dean Road.

The village of Yorkley is around 2 miles west of Blakeney. Running north through the woods at Yorkley Bottom – on the west side of the village – are the trackbed and remains of the Severn and Wye Railway's Mineral Loop, which served the collieries in the central Forest area. To the north of Yorkley and east of Parkend the line passed through the 502-yard-long tunnel at Moseley Green. The tunnel was requisitioned by the Ministry of Works as an ammunition store in 1942, and by the end of the Second World War, all the collieries served by the line had closed. In 1953 the Mineral Loop was closed, apart from the section between Pillowell and Whitecroft, which closed in 1957. The tunnel portals have been bricked up. Part of a viaduct that carried the Mineral Loop still stands to the east of Wesley Road at Pillowell, but is very overgrown and not easily accessed. The southern pier of the viaduct originally had an unusual spiral brick chute that curved around the abutment to the stream below, though how much of this survives is uncertain.

The railway station at Whitecroft, just over a mile south-west of Yorkley, is a stop on the Dean Forest Railway heritage line that runs between Parkend and Lydney Junction. The original station opened in 1875, with the start of passenger services on the Severn and Wye

Railway from Lydney Junction to Drybrook Road. Passenger services were withdrawn in 1929, although the line was used for goods services until 1966. Following restoration work, the Dean Forest Railway heritage line reopened the station to passengers in 2012.

Once the industrial heart of the Forest, the village of Parkend, around a mile north of Whitecroft, had several tramway branches converging upon it before the coming of the railway network. In 1868 the Severn and Wye Railway reached Parkend, opening a station there in 1875. It closed to passengers in 1929, however, and to goods in 1966, although mineral trains continued to run through the site occasionally until 1976. After extensive renovation and reconstruction the station was in 2006 officially reopened by HRH the Princess Royal. The station is now the terminus on the 4.5-mile-long heritage line between Lydney and Parkend. The level crossing gates at the north end of the station are said to be the longest in the UK.

Soudley village is around 5 miles to the north-east of Parkend. Tramway Road, running west, follows the course of a tramway from Bullo Pill – completed in 1814 – to Bilson and Churchway. It follows the Cinderford Valley northward through Upper Soudley, Cinderford Bridge and Bilson to Churchway. It was taken over by the Great Western Railway – who rebuilt it in broad gauge between 1851 and 1854 – and a passenger service began on the line in 1907, with Upper Soudley, Staple Edge and Ruspidge each having halts on the line. The line closed to passengers in 1958, although goods traffic continued until closure of the branch in 1967. The line was lifted within a couple of years, although

The former Ruspidge Halt.

even today its course can be easily followed. There is no longer any trace of the halts, although the former Ruspidge Halt is marked by a section of the old platform, together with the name board and two Great Western Railway-style seats. It can be found near the junction of the B4226 and B4227 roads, to the east of the Dilke Memorial Hospital.

Coleford's Speech House is around 5 miles north-west of Soudley. A Severn and Wye Railway branch running from a little north of Parkend and on to Coleford was opened in 1875. After climbing a steep gradient, the line reached Speech House Road railway station, around a mile to the south-west of Speech House. The line closed in 1963 and today there is no trace of the station buildings, although the old trackbed is a popular cycle-way and footpath. A notice 'Speech House Road Station' marks the site of the railway station, which is close to the B4226 road at the point where the cycle-way leads to Cannop Ponds.

Cannop Ponds are around a mile and a half south-west of Speech House. A stone-cutting works at an area called Stonyhill Green, close to the southern-most end of the lower of the Cannop Ponds and next to the B4234 road, is near to the start of an interesting 3-mile walk known as the Bicslade Tramroad Trail. A track runs alongside the stoneworks and continues across the main road, then along the southern edge of Barnhill Plantation, running up the steep, tree-lined Bixslade valley. This track follows the course of the Bixslade Tramroad – even though it is situated in the Bixslade valley, the Severn and Wye Railway called it the *Bic*slade Tramroad. It was opened in 1812 as a tramway for horse-drawn wagons, and

Site of Speech House Road station, Coleford.

ran between Bicslade Wharf (now renamed Cannop Wharf) and Bixhead Quarry, near Broadwell, and served a number of quarries and mines along its route. Virtually the entire route of the former tramroad is today a footpath open to the public.

In 1812 the Monmouth Railway opened a horse-drawn tramway that transported coal, clay and lime from Howler's Slade, through Broadwell – a couple of miles north-west of Cannop Ponds – and on into Coleford. It then went down the valley to Redbrook, where a spur took the tramway to a tinplate works at Upper Redbrook, while the main tramway line continued downhill to its terminus at Mayhill, Monmouth. The arrival of steam locomotive power, however, was soon to bring about the tramway's demise. The Coleford, Monmouth, Usk and Pontypool Railway came to Monmouth in 1857 and this, together with the Ross and Monmouth Railway in 1873 and the Wye Valley Railway in 1876, brought about a rapid decline in use of the tramway. It was relatively little used after 1850 and its track had been removed by 1880. It was re-laid along parts of the route by the Great Western Railway in 1883, however, when a railway was completed from Monmouth to Coleford. At Coleford, a road named 'The Tramroad', which leads off St John's Street, close to its junction with the B4228, follows part of the tramway's course through the town and is delineated by stone blocks that replicate the original tramway.

In the later years of the nineteenth century Coleford was connected to both the Severn and Wye Railway (running to Parkend and Lydney) and the Great Western Railway (running to Monmouth). Both companies had stations in the town, although they closed

Bixslade tramroad.

The course of the tramway at Coleford.

Former GWR goods shed, Coleford.

in 1967, with no trace of the buildings remaining, although the approximate line of the trackbed into the station site is now part of a pedestrian and cycle-way from Coleford to Parkend. The Great Western Railway goods shed has survived, however, and now houses a railway museum. Close to the town centre, it is accessed by following Old Station Way into Railway Drive. A nice remnant of the former Coleford to Monmouth railway line can be seen at the south-west edge of the town, where Newland Street starts to reach open countryside. A skewed rusticated stone railway bridge with a brick arch, built around 1883, crosses the road at this point.

Redbrook, on the course of the tramway and near the border with Wales, is around 4 miles west of Coleford. At the foot of the spur that ran down to the valley bottom an angled stone bridge that once took coal wagons to the village's tinplate works can be seen carrying the former line over the road.

The Wye Valley Railway between Chepstow and Monmouth opened in 1876, with a station at Upper Redbrook, where the line crossed from Wales to the Gloucestershire bank of the River Wye. The line closed in 1964 and the station was demolished in the late 1960s, with no trace surviving. The impressive cast-iron bridge, on four pairs of substantial pillars, still stands, however, and includes a footway allowing access to an attractive riverside pub, The Boat, just inside Monmouthshire.

Around 5 miles south of Redbrook, St Briavels station, on the Wye Valley Railway, was built in 1876 and remained open until 1959. Situated 2 miles from the village centre, and

Inclined tramway bridge, Redbrook.

The disused Wye Valley Railway bridge, Redbrook.

standing on the Monmouthshire side of the River Wye, close to Bigsweir Bridge, it had the distinction of being in a different country to that of the village it served. The disused station still exists, hidden by trees alongside the A466.

The small town of Lydney is around 6 miles south-east of St Briavels. Opened in 1879, a wrought-iron single-track railway bridge, which crossed the River Severn between Lydney and Sharpness, was primarily used to transport coal from the Forest of Dean to Sharpness Docks. A very impressive structure of twenty-two spans, it was in 1960 seriously damaged in a disaster when two tanker barges on the Severn near Sharpness collided and smashed into one of the bridge's pillars, causing a partial collapse. Demolition of the bridge was finally completed in 1970. A memorial stone commemorating five men who lost their lives in the accident can be seen at Lydney Docks.

The town remains on the railway network, however, and has in recent years recovered a lost railway line and station. The Dean Forest Railway heritage line between Lydney and Parkend follows part of the route of the former Severn and Wye Railway, which opened in 1875. Lydney Junction station remained open until 1964, but was subsequently demolished. In 1995, however, the Dean Forest Railway erected a new shelter at the site and, after thirty years of closure, the station was reopened. In addition to the Lydney Junction station, the Severn and Wye Railway opened Lydney Town station in 1875, conveniently located in the town centre. Passenger services

Severn Bridge disaster memorial, Lydney.

came to an end in 1960, following the serious damage to the Severn Railway Bridge, and the station closed in 1967. A new station was rebuilt on the site, however, when Dean Forest Railway's preservation work saw the line reopened through Lydney. It was officially opened in 2001.

6. Crime and Punishment

The following summary of crime in the Forest deals with events through the centuries, rather than by location, as in earlier sections. Since the Forest of Dean, and indeed Gloucestershire as a whole, is a relatively low crime area, the time period is considered more significant than any specific location.

Plump Hill at Mitcheldean must have been a desolate spot in the eighteenth century. It is said that a gibbet once stood on the hillside as a grim warning to wrongdoers, while another version says the gibbet stood at Pingry Tump to the north of Plump Hill. In 1723 one Eli Hatton was convicted of murder in the village and was executed, his body then being hung in chains at the gibbet, which was for years afterwards known as 'Eli's Post'. A further gibbet existed outside Coleford's Speech House, centuries ago, in connection with the Verderers Court. In ancient times the Verderers were empowered to pronounce

The stocks at Huntley.

sentence of death for very serious crimes. The practice of gibbeting was not outlawed in England until 1834, with the last public hanging taking place in 1868. Less serious offenders were often made to suffer pain and humiliation by having their feet restrained in stocks. In the centre of Huntley, the village stocks were originally situated on the main Ross Road, but have been re-set in the recreation ground. Commonly used from medieval times, the last recorded use of stocks as punishment in the UK was in 1872.

Many families living in the Forest existed on the verge of famine during the eighteenth century, when inflation, poor harvests and a shortage of grain led to bread becoming extremely scarce. Various disturbances in the district came to be known as 'the bread riots' and in 1795 there were cases of grain and wheat being stolen by groups of Foresters at Lydbrook and Awre. The ringleaders were captured, with several being hanged. The plight of the starving Forest of Dean people was eventually acknowledged by the Crown and £1,000 worth of corn was distributed. Although this alleviated the immediate need, a survey in 1801 found that of 3,282 foresters, only 155 were not in dire need.

In 1808 an Act of Parliament was passed permitting the enclosure of 11,000 acres of the Forest's woodland. Increasingly, too, industrialists exploited the Forest's iron and coal reserves, so that the land on which Free Miners sought a living was no longer available to them. Their traditional rights, granted by Edward I in the fourteenth century, confer that any man aged twenty-one or above and born within the Hundred of St Briavels who has worked in a local mine for a year and a day is entitled to mine for coal anywhere in that location.

In 1831 a rebellion took place at Parkend. Around 200 Foresters, led by local man, Warren James – known as 'Champion of the Forest' – set about the destruction of fences enclosing

Littledean Jail.

the forest. James urged others to join in the recovery of their rights and within a few days around a third of the fences had been destroyed. Troops attended the scene and the rebellion was quelled, with many of the Foresters escaping. Others were caught and imprisoned, however, and Warren James was subsequently sentenced to death. This was commuted to transportation for life and he was sent to Van Diemen's Land (Tasmania). James was pardoned in 1836, but he never returned home and died at Hobart, Australia, in 1841.

Poaching and sheep stealing were for many years serious problems in the area. On one night in 1861 Sergeant Samuel Beard of Littledean was watching for sheep thieves near Speech House at Coleford when he was attacked by a gang. He received severe injuries, from which he died a few days later, thus becoming the first Gloucestershire Constabulary officer to be murdered on duty. The four men were subsequently arrested and convicted, receiving lengthy penal servitude sentences. Sergeant Beard is buried in Littledean churchyard.

DID YOU KNOW?

Over a period of many years numerous reports of big cat sightings in the Forest have been made to the police. Sightings made by Forestry Commission rangers using thermal imaging cameras in 2002 and 2005 were considered particularly credible, suggesting the wild boar population may be having to share their turf with leopards or panthers. The origin of these alien animals may be the illegal release of captive species when the Dangerous Wild Animals Act was enforced in the 1970s.

One of the Forest's most enduring tales concerns two performing bears that were killed at Ruardean in the nineteenth century. Although the account has become a part of Forest of Dean folklore, the facts of the incident are all too true. Four Frenchmen were travelling around the Forest in 1889 with two muzzled and chained black bears, which performed dancing displays for the enthusiastic crowds that gathered. Following a well-received display at Cinderford, the troupe headed for Ruardean, but a false and malicious rumour had in the meantime begun to circulate, in which it was claimed a woman or child had been killed in Cinderford, with a further woman having been badly mauled.

The procession following the Frenchmen and bears became joined by an angry mob of men from Cinderford, who began attacking the animals and their keepers, following them to Ruardean – all the while beating them with makeshift weapons and pelting them with stones. Several of the terrified Frenchmen managed to escape, although the bewildered and frightened bears were less fortunate: one was beaten to death, the other – weakened by the persistent attacks – was shot and had its throat cut.

The shameful episode resulted in thirteen men being heavily fined at Littledean Police Court. A subsequent appeal succeeded in raising a substantial sum to recompense the Frenchmen, although they were probably haunted by memories of the assaults and killings for years afterwards. The Ruardean residents, for their part, had done their best to help the Frenchmen, offering them shelter and nursing their injuries. Although the attackers were from Cinderford, it was the innocent villagers of Ruardean who were for many years unjustly ridiculed and taunted with cries of 'who killed the bears?'

Quite a busy little village, Blakeney has not always been the pleasant, law-abiding place seen today. In the 1890s many inhabitants in the area were being terrorised by a gang from Blakeney Hill, with the problem becoming so persistent that eight additional officers were sent to police the village. In 1895 one such officer, PC Newport, was attacked by members of the gang and would almost certainly have been killed, but was saved when colleagues went to his aid.

The neighbouring village of Viney Hill was equally lawless in the late nineteenth century and a brutal incident of 1895 resulted in a police officer being killed in the line of duty. On 10 November of that year a group of young men who had been drinking at various pubs in Blakeney were making their way home when they met Sergeant William Morris and Police Constable Cornelius Harding at Viney Hill. There was a scuffle and both officers were struck by stones. Seriously injured, PC Harding was knocked unconscious and Sergeant Morris sustained a broken neck and a fractured skull. He died from his injuries, leaving a widow and three young children. The assailants, who were from Whitecroft and Pillowell, were arrested and charged with murder and attempted murder, going on to be convicted of manslaughter. Sergeant Morris is buried in the churchyard at nearby Lydney.

By the twentieth century the sense of disorder and willingness to assault those in authority had diminished. In the late 1920s, however, the small Forest of Dean settlement of Ellwood became the focus of local and national attention, following the untimely death of a local man. In 1924 Beatrice Pace and her husband, Harry, a quarryman who kept a flock of sheep to provide additional income, came to live in Rose Cottage, Fetter Hill, Ellwood. Outwardly, the marriage seemed happy enough but, according to Beatrice and the family children, Harry Pace was a bad-tempered, oppressive man prone to physical violence. Indeed, following threats and violence towards his wife and children, he was in 1927 reprimanded by the Coleford police sergeant. Furthermore, Harry Pace was reputedly a sexual predator and had indecently assaulted local women.

In May 1927, Harry Pace developed stomach pains and occasionally vomited blood. His doctor diagnosed gastric ulcer or gastritis and prescribed bismuth and soda. Within a month, however, Pace's condition had deteriorated. During this period he and his wife dipped his sheep to protect them from infestation by parasites. The solution used was mixed with a powder obtained from a local chemist – a powder that contained arsenic.

Within a couple of months Pace's health had considerably worsened, to a point where he was unable to stand and had no feeling in his hands. He was hospitalised, one doctor surmising that he was suffering arsenic poisoning resulting from exposure to sheep dip. Pace improved somewhat while in hospital, returning home soon

Rose Cottage, Fetter Hill, Ellwood.

after admittance, where he further improved and was gradually able to walk again. Unfortunately for Beatrice and the children, his improving health was accompanied by violent mood swings, and on Christmas Day 1927 he threatened to kill them. On Boxing Day, following this outburst, he again became very ill, vomiting and suffering stomach cramps, and his condition worsened over the days that followed. Suffering great pain, he got weaker and weaker and died just over a fortnight later, on 10 January 1928. His death was certified as the result of influenza, gastroenteritis, peripheral neuritis and anuria.

Pace's brother, Elton, however, was not satisfied with this and went to the police at Coleford, stating he did not accept that his brother had died from natural causes. Perhaps unsurprisingly, rumours began to circulate locally, suggesting that Beatrice Pace had poisoned her husband. The planned funeral was stopped by order of the police and a subsequent post-mortem examination revealed that Pace had died from arsenic poisoning. Pace's body was buried at Clearwell cemetery and the police began their investigations, Scotland Yard eventually being called in. They took numerous statements and conducted a number of interviews with Beatrice Pace and other members of the family and immediate circle.

Medical opinion at the subsequent inquest was that Pace had taken arsenic for a period of at least two to three weeks and that it was not possible for anyone to absorb sufficient poison from immersion in sheep dip to cause illness. Beatrice was asked how she thought the arsenic had got into her husband's body and she simply replied, 'I cannot tell you, I cannot tell you.' The coroner's jury found that Harry Pace had met his death by poison administered by Beatrice Pace. She was charged with murder and her trial began at Gloucester Assizes on 2 July 1928. Over the days of evidence and cross-examination that followed, Beatrice Pace attracted much sympathy, being cheered by the gathering crowds. Numerous donations were made to a fund set up to pay for her defence, and following evidence of Harry Pace's cruelty and infidelity, crowds around the court became even more enthusiastic in their support for Beatrice and mounted police had to be called in to keep order.

Following the conclusion of the prosecution's case, the defence submitted that there was no case to put before the jury, there being no evidence of administration of poison by Beatrice Pace. The minimum standard of proof against her had not been satisfied and the presiding judge directed the jury to return a verdict of 'not guilty'. This was greeted with cheers from the crowds around the court and much local and national approval. Beatrice went to live in Gloucester, and then to Wales, later returning to see out her days in Stroud. She died in 1973.

The case remains a mystery to this day. Although Harry Pace dipped his sheep in a solution that contained arsenic, that does not explain how his body contained such a large amount of the poison. Certainly, Beatrice had plenty of opportunity to administer poison and many might say more than enough motive. Her husband was undoubtedly a most unpleasant individual and, at the trial, witnesses for the prosecution proved unreliable – far from assisting the case for the prosecution, their evidence served only to increase public support for the accused. Whether or not Beatrice did in fact kill Harry Pace will forever be uncertain. It is clear, however, that the 'not guilty' verdict was met with widespread approval.

A murder committed at Lydney in 1964, in which a local resident named Peter Thomas was killed when his assailant dealt him a fatal karate chop to the throat, is significant in the use of entomology to assist criminal investigations. The victim's body was found in a Berkshire wood, having been dumped there by Hampshire man William Brittle, to whom Thomas had recently lent £2,000. When arrested and questioned, Brittle stated he had been to Lydney and repaid the loan, but there was no evidence that any sum of money had been received. The date of his visit to Lydney, and the estimated date on which the body had been dumped – deduced by pathologist Professor Keith Simpson, resulting from his study of maggots on the corpse – were one and the same. The prosecution's case rested, to a large extent, on the pathologist's entomological expertise, which was sufficiently convincing for Brittle to be found guilty of murder and sentenced to life imprisonment.

The village of Kempley, at the northern edge of the district, has unfortunate associations with the criminal and horrific activities of serial killer Fred West, who, together with his evil wife, Rose, carried out numerous murders between 1972 and 1994 at the marital home in Gloucester's Cromwell Street. The buried remains of two of his victims were found in 1994 at Fingerpost Field and Letterbox Field in the village. West was born in the neighbouring Herefordshire village of Much Marcle, a couple of miles north-west of Kempley.

A bizarre and disturbing crime took place at Bream in 2007, with three local people – who had kept a half-starved, epileptic man imprisoned in a garden shed at their home – receiving significant prison sentences. Their twenty-nine-year-old victim had been beaten, burned, tortured, and fed only on scraps, subsequently being found dead at the house in Badgers Way by paramedics who had been called to the scene. The man's abusers were convicted of falsely imprisoning and assaulting him, there having been insufficient evidence to support a more serious charge.

7. Notable Residents

Of special interest in the churchyard at Churcham is the grave of Alfred Henry 'Harry' Hook, who was born at the village in 1850. He served as a private soldier with the 24th Regiment of Foot (later the South Wales Borderers), during the Anglo-Zulu War in 1879 displaying gallantry at Rorke's Drift, for which he was awarded the Victoria Cross. Private Hook's courageous actions are immortalised on the silver screen in the 1964 epic war movie *Zulu*, in which he is portrayed by the actor James Booth.

The village of Dymock and the valley of the River Leadon proved irresistible to a number of young poets in the years leading up to the First World War. Cheshire-born Lascelles Abercrombie arrived in 1911, the tranquil surroundings inspiring him to pen some of his most memorable works. Rupert Brooke and John Drinkwater arrived soon after, closely followed by Hexham-born Wilfred Gibson. By 1914 this talented gathering was augmented by the arrival of American Robert Frost and London-born

Grave of Corporal Alfred Henry Hook VC at Churcham.

Edward Thomas. In 1914 Lascelles published a quarterly collection of poems by the Dymock poets. Entitled *New Numbers*, it included some of their best-loved poems. It was too good to last, though, and the outbreak of war scattered the poets. Gibson returned to America, Brooke died of blood poisoning in 1915 en route to Gallipoli, and Thomas was killed at Flanders in 1917. Abercrombie and Drinkwater survived the war and, together with Robert Frost, occasionally returned to Dymock to recall the happy and idealistic grouping of talented young poets. Their poetry remains much loved and a permanent exhibition about the 'Dymock Poets' can be seen in the Church of St Mary.

An end-of-terrace house close to the market house at Newent was the birthplace in 1929 of pioneering 1960s record producer Joe Meek. He enjoyed notable success with singles such as John Leyton's 1961 UK chart-topping *Johnny Remember Me* and 1962's transatlantic chart-topping single *Telstar* by The Tornadoes (written by Meek). As his success waned in the mid-1960s, however, he fell into debt and depression. It all came to a sordid and sorry end in 1967, when he murdered his landlady with a shotgun before turning the gun on himself.

The village of Kilcot, near Newent, was once home to English opera and choral music composer Rutland Boughton. He lived at Kilcot Cottage, Beavan's Hill, from 1927 until his death in 1960, producing some of his finest work there. Beavan's Hill

Joe Meek blue plaque, Newent.

has a Gloucestershire postal address but is actually on the county boundary between Gloucestershire and Herefordshire.

The seventeenth-century timber-framed Old House, north-west of the church at Lydbrook, is reputed to be the childhood home of the Brecon-born eighteenth-century actress Sarah Siddons, famous for her dramatic and expressive portrayal of characters such as Lady Macbeth.

Brierley was the birthplace in 1914 of Winifred Foley, author in 1974 of the evocative *A Child in the Forest*. She went on to write several other books centred on the Forest of Dean, as well as a few novels. She lived for some time at Huntley, later moving to Clifford's Mesne and, finally, Cheltenham. She died in 2009.

For such a small and relatively little-known town, Cinderford has had a surprising impact on the music charts. Veteran disc jockey Sir Jimmy Young, born at the town in 1921 or 1923 (biographies vary), is of course best known as a mainstay of BBC radio between 1967 and 2002. Earlier he had enjoyed UK number 1 hit singles with *The Man from Laramie* (1954) and *Unchained Melody* (1955). At the other end of the music spectrum, alternative dance band EMF, formed at Cinderford in 1989, achieved several UK hit singles in the 1990s, including *Unbelievable* (1990) and *I'm a Believer* (1995). Both of these records achieved a number 3 chart placing and 'Unbelievable', in particular, became a worldwide hit, reaching number 1 in the USA.

Old House, Lydbrook.

According to sixteenth-century historian John Foxe, author of *Actes and Monuments*, more commonly known as Foxe's Book of Martyrs, Westbury-on-Severn was the birthplace of the martyr James Baynham, youngest son of Sir Alexander Baynham, Sheriff of Gloucestershire in 1497, 1501 and 1516. Residing in London, James Baynham was a lawyer who believed in Protestant reform and extolled William Tyndale's translation of the Bible from Latin to English. He soon fell foul of Sir Thomas More, Lord High Chancellor of England, and was seized and detained by him in his house at Chelsea.

Baynham was scourged and told to name his associates. This he declined to do, despite being tortured on the rack in the Tower of London. Finally he recanted, but within a month had resumed proclaiming his religious beliefs. This could have only one end. He was burned at the stake as a heretic at Smithfield in 1531. As he burned, he is supposed to have said, 'In this fire I feel no more pain than if I were in a bed of down: but it is to me as sweet as a bed of roses.'

One of Gloucestershire's First World War poets, F. W. Harvey, spent the later years of his life at Yorkley, where he died in 1957. Earlier, as a young man, he had lived at Minsterworth.

The playwright and dramatist Dennis Potter, whose television serials included *Pennies from Heaven* (1978) and *The Singing Detective* (1986), was born at Berry Hill in 1935 and spent most of his life in the area. He died at Ross-on-Wye in 1994.

Coleford has produced several significant and highly regarded figures. Mary Howitt (née Botham), poet and author of numerous books in the nineteenth century, was born in the town in 1799. She began writing verse at an early age, one of her best-known works being the children's cautionary rhyme 'The Spider and the Fly', published in 1829. She died in Rome in 1888.

Pioneering metallurgist Robert Mushet was born at Coleford in 1811, the youngest son of ironmaster David Mushet. Robert Mushet was acclaimed for improving upon inventor Henry Bessemer's process for making steel from molten pig iron, making it suitable for industrial use, and was in 1876 awarded the Bessemer Gold Medal by the Iron and Steel Institute. He died in Cheltenham in 1891 and is buried in the cemetery there.

The heroism of South Wales Borderers soldier Captain Angus Buchanan, born at the Old Bank House, Coleford, in 1894, was recognised when in 1917 he was awarded the

Victoria Cross for his 'most conspicuous bravery' at Mesopotamia in 1916. He had, when in open ground and under heavy machine-gun fire, assisted in carrying a wounded man to cover, immediately returning to bring in another wounded comrade under heavy fire. He had just a few months earlier been awarded the Military Cross for his actions at Gallipoli. In 1917 he suffered a severe head wound as a result of sniper fire and was hospitalised in India. Unfortunately, his sight could not be saved and he remained blind for the rest of his life. After the war he became a much-respected solicitor in the town. In recognition of his bravery, Coleford residents raised a sum of money, which he asked be used to create somewhere for children to play. Thus the Angus Buchanan Recreation Field was opened in 1919. He died in 1944 and is buried in the cemetery next to the field that bears his name.

Edna May Healey, Baroness Healey (née Edmunds), was born in Coleford in 1918 and went on to marry Labour politician Denis Healey in 1945. A lecturer, documentary film-maker, historian and author of a number of books, she became Baroness Healey in 1992 when her husband received a life peerage. She died in 2010, aged ninety-two, having been married to Denis Healey for sixty-four years.

It is particularly noteworthy that Clearwell was the birthplace in 1896 of war hero and former colliery worker Private Francis George Miles of 5th Battalion, The Gloucestershire Regiment. At France in 1918, during the final weeks of the First World War, he found his company being held up by a line of enemy machine guns in a sunken road.

Grave of Captain Angus Buchanan VC at Coleford.

Grave of Francis George Miles VC at Clearwell.

Under exceptionally heavy fire, he went forward alone, located a machine-gun post and put it out of action by shooting the gunner. He then went forward alone to another post, shot the machine-gunner and captured the team of eight. He signalled to his company, who, following his initiative, were able to capture sixteen machine guns, one officer and fifty other ranks. In recognition of this act of most conspicuous bravery he was in 1919 invested with the Victoria Cross by King George V at Buckingham Palace. Francis Miles died in 1961 and is buried in the cemetery at Clearwell. A commemorative plaque can be seen on the side of his home at Lower Cross, overlooking Clearwell's recreation ground in Pingry Lane, with a further commemorative plaque being unveiled on the cemetery wall in 2018.

Lydney-born composer, organist and teacher Herbert Howells (1892–1983) wrote *The Hymnus Paradis* in 1938, following his nine-year-old son's tragic death from polio in 1935. It has come to be regarded as one of the greatest pieces of English choral music. His ashes are buried in Westminster Abbey.

Sources and Acknowledgements

Hart, Cyril, *The Industrial History of Dean* (David & Charles, 1971)

Herbert, N. M. (Ed), *Victoria History of the County of Gloucester, Volume 5* (Oxford University Press, 1996)

Phelps, Humphrey, *The Forest of Dean* (Alan Sutton, 1982)

Palmer, Roy, *Folklore of Gloucestershire* (Tempus, 2001)

Paar, H. W., *The Severn and Wye Railway* (David & Charles, 1963)

Paar, H. W., *The Great Western Railway in Dean* (David & Charles, 1965)

Sindrey, Geoff & Heath, Ted, *A Forest Beat* (Black Dwarf Publications, 2000)

Verey, David & Brooks, Alan, *Gloucestershire 2: The Vale and the Forest of Dean* (Yale University Press, 2002)

Walters, Brian, *Ancient Dean and the Wye Valley* (Thornhill Press, 1992)

Bristol and Gloucestershire Archaeological Society: Transactions

Forest of Dean Local History Society: *The New Regard*

Gloucestershire Society for Industrial Archaeology: Newsletters and Journals

The Forester